SELF-LOVE

FOR

SMALL-TOWN GIRLS

ALSO BY LANG LEAV

SELF-LOVE

FOR

SMALL-TOWN GIRLS

LANG LEAV

Andrews McMeel
PUBLISHING®

Andrews McMeel Publishing
a division of Andrews McMeel Universal
1130 Walnut Street, Kansas City, Missouri 64106

www.andrewsmcmeel.com

23 24 25 26 27 MCN 10 9 8 7 6 5 4 3 2 1

ISBN: 978-1-5248-7876-4

Library of Congress Control Number: 2022951138

Cover illustration Ed Hodgkinson

Editor: Patty Rice
Art Director/Designer: Diane Marsh
Production Editor: Dave Shaw
Production Manager: Shona Burns

ATTENTION: SCHOOLS AND BUSINESSES
Andrews McMeel books are available at quantity
discounts with bulk purchase for educational, business, or
sales promotional use. For information, please e-mail the
Andrews McMeel Publishing Special Sales Department:
sales@amuniversal.com.

For every girl who has ever wanted to go somewhere.

My dearest readers,

During the past year, I have learned to pace myself, both in my everyday life and on paper. I have come to appreciate the beauty of simplicity, to allow things to unravel in their own time. After letting so much of the outside world in for so long, I have chosen to turn inward, toward a long, protracted period of self-reflection and growth. During this time, I have come to accept the long and winding road to self-love is an ongoing process.

As I sit plucking memories and vignettes from the past two decades of my life, I have put together a narrative of moments that left me feeling enlightened in some small way. For this reason, *Self-Love for Small-Town Girls* is my most intimate collection of poems. Once again, I hope my stories will resonate with you and somewhere in this book, we will find ourselves on the same page.

With all my love,
Lang

Reset

I fall in step with time, graceful as I've ever been. I move in perfect alignment with the hours I keep. The world turns at a pace I can now comprehend. I have learned to see the passing of time as a gift. My days are mine now; I get a say in how I spend them. My life is beautiful because I say it is.

Self-Love for Small-Town Girls

They say in this small town, nothing ever happens here, but you happened. Like a story so good you can tell it verbatim, like the contents of Pandora's box, or a bottle smashing onto the sidewalk, you happened. For me you were the only thing that happened. I adored your mind and the way it was always in motion, like a skater skidding on thin ice, carving up what's left of winter. I adored your glorious bullet points and elaboration. I adored you. Spinning ballerinas in music boxes, spinning grocery carts in empty parking lots, spinning schemes about fast cars and the men who could get us out of here. But they only took us as far as the next town, took us for all we had and left us stranded. Left us to make our own sorry way back home. And you never stopped preaching to me about self-love, even when you despised everything to do with yourself. You told me to keep believing, even long after you had lost hope. You would say there was always something just up ahead and when you see it, you will know. *Just look for a sign.* You said it even as we were scouring the littered side streets for discarded lottery tickets, wondering if our numbers would ever come up. You said it while we were picking through trash for cigarette butts, looking for one last drag. And you never once asked me to stay when I was finally shown a way out. You never once said, *Take me with you.* And maybe it had less to do with our circumstances and an active choice I made to leave. And maybe love was there in all the time it took me to write this to you.

Eventually

We all become someone else's version of ourselves.

In Your Own Words

Tell me who you were, my love, before you were this. Tell me in your own words. You knew yourself once with the greatest conviction I had ever witnessed in anyone. You swore you would never change—not even for me. Tell me what distortions had warped your sense of self when you wandered through the house of mirrors that is your bright and brilliant mind. What refractions of light did you absorb as part of your reasoning that you are any less than you were. Who had come between us. What falsehood had separated you from yourself. How did you get so far that I can no longer reach you.

Play

There was a book I adored as a child; a book about making. It instilled in me the joy of seeing things come into being. With scissors, paper, and glue, tiny worlds were shaped by my own small hands.

As I grew, other things came along and took precedence. But now I have learned that the child in me still needs to be indulged. I have learned to respect and nourish all the parts of me that have once inhabited this loved and lived-in body, and not allow the outside world to dictate how I should be. To just be.

Fiction

The simple truth remains that I have only written about what has happened or what almost did. I may dress it in a thousand different outfits, but every word is true and everyone is me.

Customs

Flowing like the lifeblood in our veins
the sap of our ancestral tree
our customs

The bridge between worlds
The nightly prayer, the daily ruminations
The greetings and goodbyes
and the myriad of ways we say them

When we cross our fingers
Who we search for in a crowd
What we bring to the table
How we give ourselves away

How we knock on each door
How we ask to be let in
How we love

The phases of the moon
The cyclical return to ourselves
The synchronicities we catalog
The blown-out candles
and all the wishes made in secret

The customs we inherit
and those we make our own

Traps

Sometimes to hurt myself I think of every trap snapping shut at the same time. I think of broken bones and cries for help. I think of all the roses, callously stripped of their thorns. I think about all the things my mother wanted for me. And then I think of all the things she wanted for herself.

Poetry Is

Poetry is the recognition of the disparate. The arrangement of words that should not otherwise belong together, yet once put side by side leads us to question how they could have ever been apart.

Sleep Alone

If only I could sleep alone, I would be invincible. So seldom have I ever known this in my life. There was always somebody in the next room, always someone an arm's length away, breathing and dreaming.

If I didn't have this overpowering need to put body after body between myself and my loneliness, if I didn't spend so much time delaying the inevitable and learned to feel safe in my own skin, maybe then I would find the one with whom I want to dream.

The Right to Choose

Before they wheeled me into the operating theater, they asked for my signature. *Do you consent to having your ovaries removed if required?* At the time I didn't know if I wanted to be a mother.

Just as they were putting me to sleep, my mind went to that one simmering summer when my entire life was before me. I had sat on the bathroom floor, a strip of plastic in my hand, waiting for a line to appear, like a fate line impressing onto my palm. I could remember the flood of relief when it never showed, and I knew then I wasn't ready. Still, in the back of my mind, I drew comfort in the knowledge that if the result had been different, I still had a choice.

I woke up in recovery, ovaries intact. I still didn't know what that meant. But at least the choice was still there if it ever came down to it and whichever way it went, however long and hard the road; right up until the last moment, the choice was mine to make.

Uncertainty

When it's all over and done with, you can breathe a sigh of relief. Remind yourself there was nothing to worry about because everything worked out for you in the end. You can feel safe in the knowledge that the turmoil is now firmly behind you.

But when you're going through it as you are now, you don't know how it's going to turn out. You have no idea.

Tired

Things are no longer
the way they used to be
I can't get on a plane
whenever I am angry
So, I learn to leave you
in other ways

By letting the milk spoil
Allowing the roses to wilt

Between the dirty dishes
piling up in our sink
and the broken plates
scattered across the kitchen floor
I've gotten so used to seeing
my fractured self
in these ruined fragments

And you keep asking me
for pieces of your heart back
to give away to others
gambling it all
for your one last shot at
getting it right

Sometimes I can't stand this inertia
being stuck to a promise
that gets further away

Everything I love
is getting old and tired

Almost Anything

Comfort, security, companionship—
almost anything can be mistaken for love

But only if you've never been in love

Toxicity

Suck out the poison that has seeped into your life. Hack away the limb that has grown like a thorn in your side.

You never had a use for it before; you can learn to live without it again.

My mother—an avid gardener—would mercilessly cut away the disease before it took over. She'd say better to lose a leaf, a stem, a sprouting—than gamble it all.

I passed by some workmen around an old house, tearing into a wall. They said best to remove it before the rot sets in, before the worm finds its way to the core.

Two Doves

Two doves came to visit me one August. One took birdseed from my hand, the other shied away. I gave them each a name. One was bold and brash, the other nervous and wary. She was the smaller of the two.

Day after day, they came to see me. I came to expect them.

I kept the feathers they dropped like gifts. I learned to recognize the soft cooing of their voices, knew when they were close.

I saw them sketched in storybooks, caught glimpses of them in scripture, marveled at their likeness sculpted above my best friend's wedding cake. They say that doves are monogamous. Always, I saw them as a pair.

Until one day, only one showed up. I knew which one it was. She was such a shy, nervous thing. Flitting around me, still unsure. And then, for the first time, she put her head into my palm and let me stroke her soft, feathered head.

I thought of how every living thing dies alone. And I wondered if it was better to grasp the meaning of loss while I still had everything to lose. Or if I would prefer loss remain incomprehensible up until the aftermath.

Manifestation

You attract what you write

All Your Tomorrows

This is the recalibration of your soul, the moment of its resurrection. This is the clear, indisputable break between past and present. Your heart, mind, and breath fall into perfect alignment. Your feet stand at the threshold, ready to step into your purpose. Your hands are primed for the gathering of all your tomorrows. Every atom of your body is straining forward, working in perfect harmony with the clarity of your intent. Here is the moment of your arrival. Let yourself in.

The Language of Flowers

In the time of Victoria
they spoke the language of flowers
Appointed each multihued bloom to its subtext
Such as red for passion, fever, and fervor
yellow for friendship, spelt disappointment

In the time of Victoria
there were things that could not be said
Instead of *I love you*, they said here's a red rose
Instead of *I miss you*, here is a bouquet

In the age of Elizabeth, I say look over here
Look to the row of death lilies potted by my window
lily white lies with their muted kindness
Now look over there, I point at the sagging credenza—
to where a hand-blown vase rests, bereft and tired
holding all the weight of your silence

Only Good Things

Your love warms me the way I am warmed by the residual heat of the sun, a faraway benevolent love wishing only good things for me, the desire to see me grow without having to play a part in it.

Growth

Think of a moment in your life. A singular fragment of your life.
How do you feel about it now?
How did you feel about it then?

Days

On Tuesdays you write poetry for yourself and Thursdays you teach yourself to trust again. And you don't quite get there but you know like the day, everything passes if you wait long enough. Fridays are for saying the things you've been holding back all week long and Mondays you forgive yourself for not saying them. Wednesday comes too quickly and gives you over to what is next, a day spent wishing someone there— anyone, even for a second, as you look around the empty room filled with beautiful things, ticking off what you would trade. Sunday you help yourself to anything that is on offer, that is there for the taking. Even if it feels like it's too much. Every other day you help yourself.

The Way You Write

You do not speak the way you write
If you did, you would not know
how to keep your heart from anyone
not know how to hold back

There are some things that should
not be put together

Such as hope and indecision
love and self-worth
gasoline and fire—
my name and yours

Boundaries

Young love is clean; it doesn't require you to give up so much of yourself. You get to keep the imperfect lines that define you. You are still unaware of your boundaries because they have never been crossed.

Mediative

There is disquiet
and there is quiet
and then there is this

Not silence or quiescence
but a sense of something else

Like a song to which we half-listen
to which our pulses do not quicken

These are the in-betweens that spiral
into magnificence

Ever Speaking a Word

Is it too late to be enigmatic? To walk myself back through the twisted corridors of my life and get to where I am, have all that I have, all the while remaining unseen, without a soul ever speaking a word about me.

Acknowledgment

In a dream I was at the banquet of your life, toasting you along with everyone else. I looked on, weak with pride, glowing with love as you, always gracious, always diligent, proceeded to thank everyone but me.

Your Heart

If I had stayed with you
I would not be half the woman I am

Please understand
I had to break your heart
to follow mine

To Be You

After all the dissatisfaction and soul searching, I realized what I wanted was to be you in our relationship. I wanted someone to take care of me the way I have taken care of you.

What Would You Ask

If they said you can never have what you love, what would you ask for instead?

How You Are

While lost in a song just now, I felt you there, clear as day, stark as the blue winter sky, and I wonder if you've been talking in your sleep again about upside-down quarters and countertops and other incidentals only I would know; about apostrophes and timings, the proper order of things, and I want to ask, *Are you moving closer?*

As for me, I've been going in the way of my cored and candied heart, clanging, clamoring toward you two steps at a time. Did I miss you by overthinking things? Or was it everything else I missed? Only now do I comprehend a lifetime of procurements divided like this; between you and a third of a century, between you and my afternoons. But you know, I would trade all my days to have our time again, and I'd still be happy. Or you could break my heart all over, and you'd still be lovely.

And just when my mind begins to drift elsewhere, I hear you say, *Hey, what was the song that made you think of me?* I ask you to guess, and in guessing you tell me how you are.

Brevity

The language of my soul requires so few words. Sometimes none.

Midnight

Your name rings in the night
the clock striking twelve
your hand on the hour
I know this can't last with you

You're just a prelude
to the rest of my life
but I want to do dark things with you
before the sun comes around

In empty hallways and stairways
to radio waves and muted sounds
You want to keep me in shadow
I will wear your shame for you

Just as long as you know
I'm not yours
so you can do
whatever you want to me

Blessing in Disguise

I want you to write me a story about the emergence into light. But to make it appear as though it were happening in reverse.

Vignettes *(One)*

What hurt me most was your obliviousness. That you couldn't see past your own grandiosity, the perfectly constructed version of yourself. Whenever I tried to break through that illusion, you turned around and dressed me in it.

Vignettes *(Two)*

Never once did you consider me as anything more than a vehicle for your needs. My hunger to you was abstract. My complexity reduced to parts of others you have known.

Vignettes *(Three)*

You believed your understanding of me to be absolute when you had barely scratched the surface. There were times I peeled back the layers of skin, but I caught a glimpse of your disgust at each interval, felt reduced by your summation of me in those moments, felt myself retreating from you like a wounded animal.

Those Who Know

Let time work its magic for you, my love. For you have known the measure of what you have lost. In time, those who know can forget. Those who don't, cannot.

Culture of Silence

She was raised in a culture of silence
where the greater sin was to speak the evil
committed against her—not the evil itself

About the Sun

You lose your days the way you do when you're in love and everything around you is waking, stirring. When all the things you desire are coming to you with such astonishing ease. While you're in the thick of winter—when things are lean and hard to come by—you don't think about the sun. Even while it's shining, you forget it is there.

The Chosen One

You and I—we are the same
And yet you are the one
they have ordained
Dressed you in their
ornamental accolades

On paper they can only
tell us apart by name

Could Have Been

There was something I thought I needed from you, so I turned a blind eye when you started taking from me. What I needed from you was a place that could have been anywhere else.

What I've Kept

I'm glad I walked away from you
So, I can write you as a memory
and keep only my favorite parts

Two Souls

I am convinced I was put on this earth to know you, to see the world as you do, through your eyes if only for a moment, and to see myself and everyone through you. And in this breath of time when you and I came together, we came to life, became in essence the souls we were meant to be, forged in the same illuminating light. I was fated to see the world twice, the second time through you, both in the present and retrospectively, always in tandem. In this way, I am mine, entirely. In this way, I remain utterly yours.

Without Knowing

Who knows if a seed
Will be a flower or a weed

Who can measure the worth
Of what the dirt brings forth

Is it love or a leaf that is growing
How can I leave here without knowing

Whatever I Loved Came First

Whatever I loved came first. It was always that way for me. I never thought about what I was giving up. My love for you was the only thing that could fix me to a moment, the only thing in my life for which I have been wholly present.

To Be a Writer

To be a writer, first you must be aware of the thoughts passing through your head. That long, running monologue like a metronome ticking endlessly away, the mindless chatter. You must listen to it with all the reverence of prayer, listen closely.

Next, you must be discerning. When you hear something that breaks from that monotony, a word or a rumination that catches your breath, you must write it down. No matter where you are or what you are doing, have the discipline to write it down. The only way to hold on to this small kernel of gold is to write it down. Like the number belonging to the love of your life you once scrawled feverishly onto a napkin, you must write it down. If you don't write it down, it will be lost to you forever.

Do this for a time and it will become as easy to you as breathing. Do it for a while longer and you will be a writer.

At Your Best

Tonight, you were everything I had longed for you to be, the way you were when we first met. You shone with a light that was indomitable and I could only look on in awe. Tonight, I loved seeing you at your best even if it was for someone else.

Complex Emotions

Emotions are delicate and complex, vast and wide ranging, made up of layers upon layers of feeling, often conflicting. At times, it seems these sentiments exist purely to confuse and unsettle you. But occasionally, an emotion will seize you so completely, hold you so firmly in its grasp, that you cannot mistake it for any other thing. In these moments, you must follow its lead, go where it wants to take you. It is a directive from your heart that you cannot ignore.

Into Love

My biggest regret has never been the times when I've rationalized my way out of my love, but the instances where I'd talked myself in.

I Am Leaving

I am leaving despite knowing where you will be in the morning, looking for me among the adages and entropy, the bewildering things that pass between two people, passing through the hourglass like sand. Even though you are my world and every particle of dust that has ever the sun, I am leaving. Like the ocean, I yearn to go deeper. Like the tides, I want to rise.

You said there was nothing we could ever do to each other that could not be undone. I am leaving with this knowledge clutched tight in each fist. No one will ever love me as you have. No one will ever.

If I Stay

If I stay here with you, there will only ever be this. And this is nice; this is comfortable. This is okay, but it will never be enough.

The Rest of Your Life

At the right time, men and children can be a blessing. At the wrong time, they can rob you of something so vital that the rest of your life will pivot on this one thing. It is possible to find it with the burden of love on your shoulders, with the weight of a child in your arms, but it will be infinitely harder. So, wait, my love. There is still so much time to get everything you want. So much time to be who you are before the world shapes you into someone you're not.

How Shame Makes Us Vulnerable

Shame is easy to evoke in someone who has, oftentimes through no fault of their own, absorbed that emotion and made it their default. In the wrong environment, shame becomes a knife pointed at oneself where a mere nudge—whether or not intentional—can gravely wound.

Who I Was

There is a way for me to become the person I want to be, but first I need everyone to forget who I was.

Where Everything Is

Oftentimes I am preoccupied with where everything is, to know the placement of things. I think of my pens lined in neat rows, the words I will write with them. I think of the long, cool winter, the foghorn in the morning, the man asleep beside me, the tannins in my tea. I think of my cats sunning themselves on the front porch, photo albums, heirloom jewels and spatulas found where they were last left. The birds in the trees, chirping their amusement, the insects scurrying in the undergrowth. There is a place for everything at any given moment. The sun at a particular time of day, the moon at midnight. The hands of a clock and the voice of someone I love at the end of the line and always, always, you standing on the rain-soaked pavement, turning away. For my peace of mind, I need to know where things are, to know they are still within my reach.

Such As

You haven't said a word to me in
such a long while—
Why?

I am waiting for things to pass
Such as?

Such as my hurt
Such as your memory of me
Such as time

Invisible

I've lived with you long enough to know you don't see me as you used to. When I say this is hurting me, you say I'm being too sensitive. When I tell you I am unhappy, you answer I have no reason to be. And when I'm begging you to listen to me, really listen, you say to me, *I am*.

For a Time

For a time
we had it all
all this time
and more

When the good years
came rushing in
came to us unbidden

We had all the time
in the world
until suddenly
we didn't

Your Place

If my life were a page
you would be the place I mark
the highlight—
the line I would underline—
then circle twice
no one could ever miss
your place in my story

Loving Me

Thank you for loving me with all your good intentions and honesty; for giving me some of the happiest years of my life. For showing me that love can at once be miraculous and nurturing, for shaping me into the person I am today—one who is soft yet resilient. Thank you for allowing me time to make myself whole, to learn how to love myself again the way you have loved me all these years with such tender conviction, for never asking anything of me, for never once withholding. Thank you for loving me and for letting me go.

My Day, Today

How do I approach my day today
on a day such as this
when everything is resting
on that one thing
that swing between
all my wildest dreams and despair

Where do I start?

What would make this day
any less than what it already is
regardless of what it does to me

How do I ready myself
How can I prepare
when my life up until now
feels like one endless preparation

What more can I do
but place myself
where I'm meant to stand

And then
And then

A deep gushing breath
A small, tentative step

Have You

Have you been good to me. Have you been fair. Have you been faithful. Did you ever humiliate me. Was everyone laughing at me and I just didn't see it. Are you sorry for what you put me through. Will you make it up to me.

My Biggest Regret

You were the end of an era. The end of an error.

Almost Like That

You love the blankness of a fresh page—don't you, my dear?
A hotel room somewhere far away, billowing curtains, old
ghosts, sculpted by the breeze. You tell your new lover about
me as you slip into crisp laundered sheets. You tell her about
the first time you and I met, and you say, *This feels almost like
that*. You can't find that feeling again, not exactly, but you'll
have the scent of a new perfume to impress on your memory,
a collection of vignettes for your book of roses.

Every Scrap of It

Self-love ignites within me like lust, like indignation, in a blaze of immutable light. It shows up in the way I defend the things for which I used to make apologies. In the way I am no longer driven by the need to explain the reasoning behind my reasons. It took me so long to realize I didn't need anyone's permission to love what I had in the past, to gather up my entire life in my arms and own every last scrap of it. That the measure of my self-worth was not tied to these things.

Light

Although you cannot walk down this dark, moonless road with me, you can shine a light.

Places

We all have our hiding places. Whether it is in the crook of someone's arm, the branch of an old oak tree, or the poems we never show to a single soul. We all have places we run to, where we feel safe.

I want to be that place for you.

Inner Child

Ask your inner child, *What do you want me to do for you today?*

Give them all time in the world to answer.

And then do what they ask.

The Craft

I am often asked how I became an author. As though myself and others like me hold a key to a secret doorway. The truth is, I have never strived to *be* an author. There is hardly anything I enjoy about it. It was my love of writing that brought me into this role. Becoming an author was purely incidental to my love of words.

Writing has been the one constant in my life, as intrinsic to me as memory, as potent to me as loss. Every word I have ever written is woven into the fabric of my existence. It is not a fad, a passing interest, or a means to an end. Writing is a craft I intend to practice with all the dedication and reverence it demands. Knowing with all certainty this is what I was meant to do.

You Couldn't

It reached a point where there was nothing more I wanted from you, where I couldn't even imagine wanting you. When the only thing left you could possibly give me was closure. But you couldn't even give me that.

Good Deeds

The time and care you put into things will never go unnoticed. The universal ledger keeps count of every good deed you have done and will reward you accordingly. But only if it comes from a place of love and not obligation. With sweet gratitude and not resentment.

Meant to Love

This is the version of me that you were meant to love. How cruel it is I had to lose you to become this person.

Self-Explanatory

Today I wrote in my journal after a lengthy hiatus. The first thing I thought to write was an explanation for my absence. Isn't that strange? The need we feel to justify ourselves is so powerful that we do it even when no one is watching.

Rooms

In a room, there are three doors.

The one on the left is The Past. The one on the right is The Future. And the one in the middle is The Present.

You have a choice.

If you enter The Past, you must live your life again from a moment that is unspecified. If there is something you wish to change it may be too late. But if you choose to enter The Past, you must stay and live your life from then on. All other doors remain closed to you.

If you enter The Future, it is one that is indeterminate, a single outcome plucked from all the possibilities. It may be better than the future waiting for you now. It could be infinitely worse. The only rule is, once you step into The Future and witness firsthand the culmination of your life, you will be hurled back into the past to live out this alternate version of yourself. Despite knowing how it will end.

The final option is The Present—once you walk through that door, your life will be as it is up until now and The Future will not be known to you. There will be no chance to affect The Past, but you can build your future from this point.

What will you choose?

Attachments

I felt that things were happening without me, but somehow I was attached to those things, as though I sensed I was still part of them but couldn't tell for sure. And yet, I couldn't bear to let that part of me go, even though much of it was only in my head. I couldn't seem to separate myself entirely.

Marriage of Convenience

My parents began with a marriage of convenience that ended in love. We started with love and ended where they began.

Self-Domination

Your most dangerous self is your present self. The self that talks you out of doing what's hard in the moment. This is the self that must always be held accountable, kept in check. With time, consistent mastery of the present self will yield the best and brightest version of you.

Every Artist

Every artist dreams of languishing in their own perceived genius, separate from the world and all the prying eyes. Every artist wants to hoard their creations without the need to sell off pieces of their soul. Deep down, every artist wishes they could remain undiscovered, like buried treasure.

To Hurt

Although I was no stranger to hurt
they still found new ways to hurt me

One man used his hands
another his voice
and another used his silence

Rubber Bands

My mother said
Do not raise your children here
Among the shards of glass
broken bottles slammed
into the pavement
by men with bad intentions
stalking the streets
Gunfire ringing
into the night

A wise man once said
we are rubber bands
that can only stretch so far

Something pulls us back
against our will
And in the end
we wind up back
where we are

With Writing

My relationship with writing is sacred. The one I hold the dearest, put above all else. Still, I have betrayed this unspoken pact between us too many times to count. Yet she still loves me, still shows up for me. Makes me believe I am worthy of her grace. She keeps giving with all the generosity of one who is infinite.

A Book in His Hand

If you placed your past
like a book in his hand
Would there be parts he'd erase?

If your answer is *yes*—
you are with the wrong man

Go with Your Heart

If you go with this man because he is a good man, you will learn in time the damage that a man can do, even one who is well-meaning. What I'm trying to tell you is to go with your heart. Even if it hurts you. I'm trying to tell you there is no way to keep your heart safe, no point in trying. So, you might as well have a say in who gets to break it.

In the Present Tense

Here he is—
someone you can write about
in the present tense

and your heart is filled
with something so much
more potent than love
it is awash with hope

and here you are
the rest of your life
before you
he is all you want
for the rest of it

and this—
this new version of you—
is more than you have
ever known yourself to be
aglow with pride
abundant with feeling
bursting with words
as never before

Fluency

If I could give my mother anything, it would be a bike that we can ride in tandem, our legs, the same shape and weight, pumping away, moving us forward in the same direction. We would laugh about the same things under a sky that we have known the entire length of our lives. We would be fluent in the same language.

All I Can See

I look at you and think of how I have loved you—how much, and for how long. I look at you and already I see my past.

Attachment to a Time

I think we attach meaning to specific periods in our lives; the memories rendered during those times are often deeply imbued with portents and miracles, which we can only uncover in hindsight. Yet these are the moments that go on to shape our lives in new and unexpected ways. It seems the further away we get from those memories, the greater they grow in significance. Strange how things feel more vibrant and alive with the passing of time, when there is less of it.

Love Is Here

You hold with both hands not willing to let anything go. You leave me without ever going anywhere. You think what we had in the beginning exists in someone else. In the rush to find what you are looking for, you have stopped seeing what you already have.

Love is here—why do you go elsewhere.

Decisions

The further you get in life, the faster everything moves. You only get so much time to take everything in, to decide what to grasp, what to hold on to. There are things that you will miss. Do not spend too long on them. Sometimes, we make too much of what has gone. When life reveals itself to you, when it begins to unfold at a manic pace, you may only have a fraction of a second to make up your mind. The most important thing is that you do.

Self-Worth

I don't know why I was so afraid, I really don't. I had such a terror of being seen, being judged, held to account for all my imperfections. I hid myself behind my words, not knowing they had been exposing me all along. Imagine if I had just been comfortable in my own skin. If I knew then what is so painfully obvious to me now. There is no point in trying to please everyone. I will still be subjected to the same scrutiny, suffer the same criticisms. If only I knew not to base my self-worth on someone's idea of what I should be—if only I had arrived earlier at this simple yet profound conclusion. I could have saved myself so much time and misery. I could have saved myself.

All She Had Known

Imagine if you had been selfless. Imagine if you had not acted out of your own self-interest, projected onto her your own sad stories.

How she would have flourished under your light. How she would have thrived with every kind word. Imagine if all she had ever known from you was love.

At Peace

As I reflect on the past ten years, barely anything is recognizable. Yet with everything that has changed, there is a small, revolutionary one that has eclipsed all else. I don't know how to describe this change in me. Only since I've learned to care less, things don't feel as hard.

Women Like Me

Women like me
we don't leave
for no good reason

You read my poems now
looking for a clue

To see if I know
what you have done
and now you know I do

What You Deserve

You deserve someone who loves you in a sweet, uncompli-
cated way. Someone to whom you can tell anything, know-
ing your secrets are safe and your words will never be used
against you.

Time for Me

Everything about me is already in the past and I am glad. After I have lived such lives, it is time for me to be where I am at my most content, telling my stories in retrospect through words I have gathered along the way. To reflect on things that have been. To know for certain how things were.

On My Behalf

It's not that you didn't love me enough
But there was always something you loved more

It's not that you didn't come to my defense
But you weren't angry enough on my behalf

Past the Tidemark

Maybe it's the change in weather, but I'm thinking about you again and it doesn't take much, does it? But you know how it gets for me this time of year, how January always comes before I'm ready. Comes with all its merriment and expectation, and I always wonder, is this the year? But nothing ever changes for me even though I still cling to what you said once, how I was destined for great things and whether that has anything to do with you. I guess if it were true, there would be signs pointing me to you. I guess if it were true, I'd get to have you as well. But there are no pathways to you I see, no way of getting further than I've already been. Like a wave on a shoreline that has never gone past the tidemark.

Until Our Story Ends

Where are we on the page, my love? Can you tell. If we said goodbye now, can we ever pick up where we left off? You never really know—do you? Where you are in a story until the story ends.

Acknowledgments

I'd like to thank my agent, Alec Shane, for your support and guidance.

Kirsty Melville and the team at Andrews McMeel for bringing this book to life.

Patty Rice and Kathy Hilliard for all your help and encouragement.

Thanks to Ed Hodgkinson for lending your stunning artwork to the cover of this book.

Michael and Ollie, for taking such great care of me, and my beautiful readers to whom I owe everything.

Index

index